AN
INSPIRED LIFE

First Edition

AN INSPIRED LIFE

AMARI PRIDE

tate publishing
CHILDREN'S DIVISION

Published by Tate Publishing & Enterprises, LLC
127 E. Trade Center Terrace | Mustang, Oklahoma 73064 USA
1.888.361.9473 | www.tatepublishing.com

Tate Publishing is committed to excellence in the publishing industry. The company reflects the philosophy established by the founders, based on Psalm 68:11,
"The Lord gave the word and great was the company of those who published it."

Published in the United States of America

ISBN: 978-1-68097-185-9
1. Religion / Christian Life / Spiritual Growth
2. Poetry / Subjects & Themes / Inspirational & Religious
15.07.06

Dedicated to

My devoted husband Phillip
The memory of my loving parents
My children Robert, Deborah and William
My grandchildren Sunny, Kody, Korey, Jeramy and Kortney
My sisters Carol and Dixie
The memory of my brother Richard
My brother Terry
All the people who have helped me along the way,
many of whom have become brothers and sisters
in Christ
and all my loving family from my side and my husband's
who have all helped me become who I am today

Thank you all

PREFACE

One life among millions is but a single note amid this divine opera unfolding in a world of interconnected players. From space, we see the universe which is so vast we have never scratched the surface of understanding how it came to be. Looking inward, we see a planet where resides incalculable forms of teaming organisms, all alive, each struggling to hang onto one more micro-second of this thing we call life.

The majority of the forms of life on this miniscule dot in space rarely focus on anything outside their immediate range of awareness. Then there is man. Unlike all the other forms of life, man goes beyond feeding the belly, eliminating body waste and resting his temporal fleshly vehicle. Mankind is unique in that we go beyond exploration, beyond the touchable, dream the impossible, live in reality and imagination, cross over forbidden borders and dare to seek our origins and challenge traditions. We long for knowledge even when that means sacrificing our very existence to learn the answers. We have among us the lowest examples of reprobate scum of the earth sorry excuses for human beings. We also have among us the qualities of mercy, love, sacrifice and the highest examples of human endeavors.

We all begin life the same, an egg and a sperm gestate and a life begins. Some are born into riches with all the advantages of Royalty. Many are born into social advantage and a family who have the means to help them achieve goals set for them in their search for purpose. Others are born into uneducated working class families and remain in that caste all the days of their lives. Too many are born into poverty and hopeless despair and never rise above their meager existence and barely have enough to eat to keep their bony bodies drinking in one more breath of life. How you deal with these birth experiences depends upon which country you happen to be born into. The quality of life you have and the advantages afforded to you is limited by your place of birth and whether you can overcome the disadvantages of the obstacles that stand in your way. Without help from others, we flounder and usually fail at anything we hope to achieve. That is why we need to reach out and help each other and those who cannot help themselves. This is how we grow and learn and have value in our lives. Those in need of help may be within our sight of vision or they may be thousands of miles away, but they cannot do it alone. I am but one life among the myriads of teaming souls on this planet. I could not have survived without the help of my family and many others who have reached out and helped me in my time of need. I truly thank them all and hope to be able to one day reach out beyond my immediate world and help others who are not able to help themselves. This goal has brought me to where I am today, and is a result of having found the miracle of living an inspired life.

JOURNEY OF THE SOUL

The soul has a journey that might also be called a quest. Each of us has one and no two are alike. We are unique beings created to last forever.

This work represents The Spirit, The Living Soul. The Soul cannot be fathomed; it is bright and energetic, filled with a searching, reaching out; it is a brilliant vibrant light in the darkness.

It is not easy to pinpoint one thing about my art. It seems like I have been an artist all my life. Everything I see and do is reflected through the eyes and emotions of art.

I see life in everything and have a burning desire to capture what I see and transmit it through my art. I seek to show it as no one has ever seen before or presented in the same way. I love to take the ordinary and transform it into something beautiful and majestic. I want my

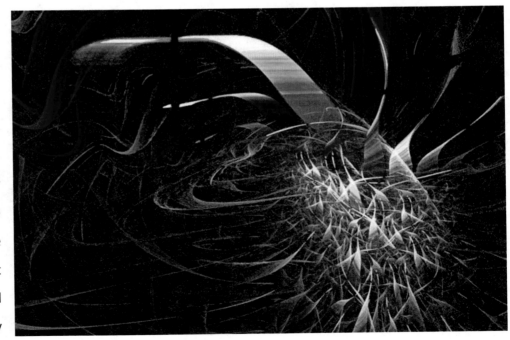

art to be an extension of myself, a unique imprint of my soul and personality, life force and life experience. All these things woven together into a magical expression that reveals the wonder and inner sight that refuses to be subdued by fear or timidity.

Our lives are like a tapestry, woven from within and without, knit together by fine threads formed from the mind of God from the very foundation of creation.

THE HEAVENS WERE MADE

Psalms 33:6: "By the word of the LORD were the heavens made; and all the host of them by the breath of His mouth."

Psalms 33:7: "He gathered the waters of the sea together as an heap: He layed up the depth in storehouses."

Psalms 33:8: "Let all the earth fear the LORD: let all the inhabitants of the world stand in awe of Him."

Psalms 33:9: "For He spoke, and it was done; He commanded, and it stood fast. "

Everything there is or ever will be was created by Jesus Christ, the Son of God, the Lord God Almighty, God the Son who also is called by many names including the Alpha and Omega, the Beginning and the Ending, the Almighty.

1 Timothy 3:16 "God was manifested in the flesh" (appeared in) 1 John 4:2; 2 John 7 "came in the flesh." 1 John 1:2: For "the life was manifested, and we have seen it, and bear witness, and shew unto you that eternal life, which was with the Father, and was manifested unto us."

1 Timothy 3:16 says it was God come in the flesh, a person, not just eternal life that was manifested. 1 John 3:8: "For this purpose the Son of God was manifested." The Bible makes it clear that specifically the person of God is the Son, He was the God who was revealed and made known.

If we go back to verse we find this. vs. 5 "And you know that HE was manifested to take away our sins." Here John is identifying the deity was made known. Who is the "He"?

John 1:2 "He was in the beginning with God all things were made through Him... In Him was life... From this we see this life is in a He, which is a person. This He was with another person and this Other made everything through Him. Again in vs.10 "He was in the world, and the world was made through Him. This is the same He and Him that is previously established to be with God, the same He in vs.1 who was with the Father. Obviously from the Scriptures, the Son, not just the Father had eternal life. He was made known, and revealed to mankind, this is the eternal life of John 1:2 that was with the Father. So we see from the Scripture that there was another person (He) that was with the Father before creation began.

This also shows the truthfulness of Jesus' prayer in John 17:5 which is not about his future humanity.

Jesus is reflecting back and praying in the present asking to be glorified as He once was with the Father before the creation. "Together WITH yourself."

This work represents the power of God and the glory of His creation.

Jesus says He was "with the Father before the world began." John the apostle said in John 1:2 He was there in the beginning with God. And John 1:10 the world was made through Him. This very same concept is written from the writer in Hebrews1 that, "God made the worlds through the Son", as well as Colossians 1:15. If He is not literally there, then it is a lie. The Bible shows these are not roles that the one God acts in, for both are there as persons, taking part in creation. In the Beginning God created the heavens and the earth.

John 1:18 states, "No one has seen God at any time. The only begotten Son who is in the bosom of the Father, he has declared Him." When was the Son with the Father in this manner, before He was incarnated, as a thought, a plan? The answer is 'No' as a person. If we change the Son to be future tense, then why not the Father too? Why does one exist before creation and not the other who is WITH Him? The Bible is clear they both literally, personally and simultaneously exist. As Pr. 30:4 asks in relation to the creative acts what is His name and what is his Sons name, if you know?

That is the Bible's final answer!

CREATION - HOW LONG DID IT TAKE?

Each day is described as "The Evening and the Morning". Although the sun, moon and stars were not created until the third day, the description of the days did not change. God authored the Bible. He created the universe and He explained how He did it. He did not need to have the sun, moon and stars in place to set the number of hours in a day since He created them according to His will and clearly stated that each of the six days of creation consisted of "An Evening and a Morning". His plan for time already existed from the conception of creation and He put each part of the plan in place to complete the whole of creation.

At the end of the 6th day, all things were created and complete and everything was good. There was no death or sin yet since everything was good. Death came into the world because of the sin of Adam which took place while God was away on the 7th day.

Romans 5:12-14: "Wherefore, as by one man sin entered into the world, and death by sin; and so death passed upon all men, for that all have sinned: For until the law sin was in the world: but sin is not imputed when there is no law. Nevertheless death reigned from Adam to Moses, even over them that had not sinned after the similitude of Adam's transgression, who is the figure of him that was to come."

1000 years does not fit scripture. Since Adam lived 900 years, he would have been dead before the 7th day even came. Adam and Eve were created on the 6th day. Archeology and science have shown a "sudden explosion" of life during what they call the Pre-Cambrian period. They have tried to find another answer but failed. Life is shown scientifically and through archeology to have been an instantaneous creation. There are no intermediate forms to be found.

The issue of sin must be dealt with right here on Earth. The fact that sin came into the world through the rebellion of Adam and Eve, means that there was no sin anywhere in the universe before then. Because of sin, death entered into the whole universe. In the book of Genesis, we find that the Heavens and the Earth were created on the 1st day. It is described as a literal 24 hour period (an evening and a morning). In the process of creation, the Earth was created days before the Sun, the Moon and the Stars giving us God's word on the importance of the Earth. We are told in Genesis 1:14 that the Sun, the Moon and the Stars were created for the Earth. There are many places in the Bible that reveal the importance of the Earth in creation. After studying the whole Bible we come to Revelation where it is revealed that all that there is in our universe will be destroyed and a new Heaven and new Earth will be created far different from what it is now. Revelation 21:1-2: "And I saw a new heaven and a new earth: for the first heaven and the first earth were passed away; and there was no more sea. And I John saw the holy city, new Jerusalem, coming down from God out of heaven, prepared as a bride adorned for her husband."

As a Christian, I have learned that God is Good, God is Righteous, God is Just and God never destroys the Righteous with the wicked. Therefore, if there were other beings on other planets who somehow fell under the curse of sin and death because of Adam and Eve's rebellion, that does not conform with the nature of the Lord God Almighty. If there were beings on other planets in other galaxies who were to be destroyed when all there is in existence now because of Adam and Eve's rebellion, as is described in Revelation 21, that also would not conform to the nature of God Almighty. One day, after all is finished, and the sin issue is dealt with, there will be a new Heaven and a new Earth, and then, perhaps there will be beings throughout the entire new Universe who will know no death, will not rebel against their creator because the lessons learned here will be taught by the Saints and Priests of God forever and forever. Then will be the victory, death and decay and sorrow and hunger and all the things that come from sin will be no more.

One more thing I find it necessary to speak about when dealing with the issue of creation. When I hear someone say that their loved ones are now an angel in Heaven watching down upon them, I so much want to reach out and tell them a very important truth...

ANGELS ARE A SEPARATE CREATION FROM MAN.

God created man a little below the angels but one day we will be higher than them scripture says.

These passages are of a dual nature, speaking of the 'Son of man' which is prophetic of the title given to Jesus Christ the Messiah and also indicating the position mankind will hold after the regeneration in the New Heavens and the New Earth.

"But one in a certain place testified, saying, what is man, that You are mindful of Him? or the Son of man, that you visit Him?" Heb. 2:6:

"You made Him a little lower than the angels; You crowned Him with glory and honor, and didst set Him over the works of Your hands:" Heb. 2:7

"Do you not know you we shall judge angels? How much more things that pertain to this life?" (1Corinthians 6:3)

Many people are not aware of these or other passages that clearly state that angels are a different creation from man. God created man (male and female) to be His companions forever which is a special place unlike any other and not even given to the angels. Man was created for far better things than to be angels and we should not be willing to settle for less that the best that God has for us. Mankind was created to be the adopted children of God. Jesus came and purchased for Himself, a Bride who is to reign with Him for eternity, a chosen people out of the whole world unlike any other. You are invited to come to the foot of the cross, confess your sins, repent and ask Jesus into your heart. When you do this, the Holy Spirit with come to live in your heart and will never desert you. God will impute the Righteousness of Jesus to you, washing away all your sins, making you a new, clean creation, whole and untarnished by the past, taking you into His family, the Bride of Christ.

"But if we walk in the light, as he is in the light, we have fellowship one with another, and the blood of Jesus Christ his Son cleanseth us from all sin. If we say that we have no sin, we deceive ourselves, and the truth is not in us. If we confess our sins, he is faithful and just to forgive us our sins, and to cleanse us from all unrighteousness. If we say that we have not sinned, we make him a liar, and his word is not in us." (1John 1:7-10)

Jesus said that there is only ONE unpardonable sin. Matthew 12:30-32: "He that is not with Me is against Me; and he that gathereth not with Me scattereth abroad. 31) Wherefore I say unto you, All manner of sin and blasphemy shall be forgiven unto men: but the blasphemy against the Holy Ghost shall not be forgiven unto men. 32) And whosoever speaketh a word against the Son of man, it shall be forgiven him: but whosoever speaketh against the Holy Ghost, it shall not be forgiven him, neither in this world, neither in the world to come." The ONE sin for which we cannot ever be forgiven is BLASPHEMY of the Holy Ghost (Spirit), that is calling the work of the Holy Spirit evil. What is the work of the Holy Spirit? It is what happens when we receive the call from God to come to the foot of the Cross and we recognize our need of a savior because we cannot save ourselves, and we confess our sins and respond to the call with a "Forgive me of my sins Lord. Yes, I believe on the Lord Jesus, and I give Jesus my sins in exchange for His robe of Righteousness." Then the Holy Spirit comes into our heart and gives us a new heart, a spiritual heart with a love of God, and we die to the old self and rise up a new creation in Christ Jesus. That is the work of the Holy Spirit. Jesus said, "Unless a man is Born Again of the Spirit, he cannot enter into the kingdom of Heaven." So, we understand that there is only one way to get to Heaven and that is by being Born Again of the Holy Spirit. When one rejects the Grace of God, effectually calling it evil, they have committed the one and only unpardonable sin. There is no other way to get into Heaven, but by embracing the Holy Spirit and believing God, Jesus is the truth, the life and the way. Eternity is a very long time, best to spend it in Heaven.

Here is another mystery God has revealed to us. Most people have totally overlooked this passage in the Bible. It is truly one we will witness one day, all creation will be a witness to this magnificent event:

Great is the mystery of God, that we will one day all witness this that is to come. After Jesus Christ has subdued all things and every knee bows and confesses He is Lord, after the Great White Throne Judgment, after the old Heaven and Earth a passed away and there is a New Heaven and a New Earth, then shall this prophecy come to pass:

"Then cometh the end, when He shall have delivered up the kingdom to God, even the Father; when He shall have put down all rule and all authority and power. For He must reign, till He hath put all enemies under His feet. The last enemy that shall be destroyed is death. For He hath put all things under His feet. But when He saith all things are put under Him, it is manifest that He is excepted, which did put all things under Him. And when all things shall be subdued unto Him, then shall the Son also Himself be subject unto Him that put all things under Him, that God may be all in all." (1Corinthians 15:24-28)

If you die today? Where will you go, HEAVEN or HELL? Don't believe in HEAVEN or HELL? Think about what IF there is a .01% chance this is correct? (Yet it is 100% correct) Where would you spend eternally?

Even when we travel 3 nights and 4 days. We'll be very concerned about where we are going to stay.

However, we are not talking about couple of days, we will live forever eternally in the universe. We are not talking 1 year, 5 years, 10 years, 25 years, 65 years, 80 years, or let's say, you lived a maximum of 100 years. Your lifetime x 1000 x 1000 = 100 million years passed away from the day you died. There you are whether you are living like the majestic sons of GOD in Glorious Heaven full of joy, peace and love or you are still burning in the flames of Hell in unbearable, immeasurable and unimaginable pains every second FOREVER WITHOUT END.

We get to CHOOSE where we get to spend eternity while we are in flesh. God in His sovereignty has given us the ability to choose life or choose death forever and ever and ever.

We can only have what God Almighty gave us, the free will and the time. When our allowed time is up, we must stand before in God's righteous Judgment to be rewarded forever or to be punished forever.

JESUS Christ (the Messiah\Savior of the world) loves, loves, loves you. He doesn't want you to perish in Hell. Everyone can be saved, everyone is invited, those who truly believe in The LORD JESUS will enter Heaven, the Kingdom of God.

JESUS is ALIVE. HEAVEN is REAL. It is the most glorious, beautiful, joyful, wonderful, full of Love place EVER. No earthly words can describe HEAVEN.

TODAY is your day of Salvation. Tomorrow may be too late.

We all know that the Earth is currently experiencing devastation unprecedented in History. Total disasters and wars will increase in The End Times.

The Good News is...

God is in total control; He allows things to happen.

Nothing is hidden from God. No one and nothing can stop God for He IS The ALMIGHTY, The ALPHA & OMEGA, The Great IAM who always has been, without beginning or ending, The Everlasting God.

He IS coming back for His true Bride, What a Glorious day it will be. Hold on to your faith, hope and love of JESUS until the end. Let no one rob you of your faith.

Many people and churches will be left behind because they have turned away from the Word of God and gone after false doctrines, worshipping the world and following other gods who are not God but are creations of the father of lies, Satan.

The day of the LORD is at hand.

Know this, even to those who are in the arms of death at this very moment, they are currently standing before God having to give an answer for themselves. Those who have the wedding Garment of Jesus (His cloak of Righteousness) will have Jesus there standing with them giving evidence that they are His and He has bought them with His blood and therefore they will not be condemned but will pass from death into life.

So I ask you again, if you died right now, this very moment, where will you spend eternity?

THE GARDEN OF GETHSEMANE

Most of my art is bold because that is how I see life, bold filled with color and light and joy. There are times when I see it softly and feel its tender muted pale wafts of whispered colors floating through my mind seeking expression. That is a wonderful thing too, all forms and colors and brightness and shadows reveal the wonder of the spirit. All these things are merely a way of expressing the glory of God. He created my spirit and gives it hope and brightness, inspiration and joy. When I consider the terrible price He paid to secure my place in Heaven, I am overwhelmed with awe and a sense of gratitude beyond any words that can even explain it. He knew, being God the Son, what lay before him on that dark night when He retreated with His Apostles to pray and prepare Himself for what was to come. The stress of the coming event caused His very pores to open and He sweated great drops of blood, and yet He endured the agony of fully comprehending the fact that He could easily speak and annihilate everyone who stood against Him, who would come for Him seeking to destroy Him that night. This is how I came up with the poem, The Angel, a poem about the events that were taking place while Jesus prayed and the Apostles fell asleep, the very Apostles who were told to keep watch lest anyone come and take them by surprise. Of course Jesus already knew the enemy was coming. This night even His Apostles were under a test, one which they, like all of us, would fail and yet they would later be so bold as to give their very lives to take the Gospel to all the world.

Jesus in the Garden of Gethsemane in prayer in the hours before His arrest and crucifixion:

Lu 22:39: "And He came out, and went, as He was wont, to the mount of Olives; and His disciples also followed him."

Luke 22:40-43: "And when He was at the place, He said to them, "Pray that you do not enter into temptation." And He was withdrawn from them about a stone's cast, and kneeled down, and prayed, saying, Father, if You are willing, remove this cup from Me: nevertheless not My will, but Your will, be done. And there appeared an angel to Him from heaven, strengthening him."

Something that we, as human beings, cannot fully fathom is that God Almighty was willing to subject Himself to the pain, rejection and humiliation for us while we were yet in our sins, and for all generations from Creation of the world.

THE ANGEL

Azure waves are melting away

giving birth to amber hues of evening.

I have nourished eager hearts

and comforted those around me.

In the light of the pale moonlight from my flesh great drops of blood now seep.

AMARI PRIDE

My body yearns for another way, exhausted in deep prayer I sink.

The path before me I have seen the cup which only I can drink.

Droplets of blood fall to the ground

as I struggle knowing what lays before me.

An eon has passed and dawn draws near and the angel is here to strengthen me.

In the distance I can hear them coming.

Now I will fulfill my destiny.

A CROWN OF THORNS AWAITS ME

Many people say they like Jesus' message of love, but they frequently completely misunderstand what Jesus' message of love really is. As John wrote, "In Him was life, and that life was the light of men. The light shines in the darkness, but the darkness has not understood it" (John 1:4-5)

Jesus does teach a message of love, but it is more than a general "let's love everybody" message or "we're all one with the universe."

It is the message of, "I love you so much that I am offering you life if you will believe in Me." It is the message that we can be reconciled to God by being "born again" through faith in Christ and entering into a personal relationship with Him. It is the core of Christianity.

If you have been taught that Jesus' message of love is no different from that taught by other religions, that all religions are one or the same, let me introduce you to His actual words, taken from the Gospel of John. Jesus' message - that belief in Him, personally, is the way to be reconciled with God. Jesus does teach a message of love, but it is more than a general "let's love everybody" message or "we're all one with the universe."

Jesus says He is the shepherd, gate, and giver of eternal life.

It is not just Jesus' message of love that counts. It is Jesus Himself! Read His words and you will see that His message is very different from those who say all religions are basically the same, that all religions are equal, or that all religions are true.

"I am the gate; whoever enters through Me will be saved. He will come in and go out, and find pasture" (John 10:9)

"I am the good shepherd. The good shepherd lays down His life for the sheep" (John 10:11)

"I give them eternal life, and they shall never perish; no one can snatch them out of My hand" (John 10:28)

Jesus said to her, "I am the resurrection and the life. He who believes in Me will live, even though he dies; and whoever lives and believes in Me will never die. Do you believe this?" (John 11:25-26)

"Put your trust in the light while you have it, so that you may become sons of light." "When He had finished speaking, Jesus left and hid Himself from them" (John 12:36)

"There is a judge for the one who rejects Me and does not accept My words; that very word which I spoke will condemn him at the last day" (John 12:48)

Jesus answered, "I am the way and the truth and the life. No one comes to the Father except through Me" (John 14:6)

"I am the vine; you are the branches. If a man remains in me and I in him, he will bear much fruit; apart from Me you can do nothing. If anyone does not remain in me, he is like a branch that is thrown away and withers; such branches are picked up, thrown into the fire and burned" (John 15:5-6)

Are all religions the same? Jesus says that belief in Him opens the gate. It's important to realize what "believe" means. It means much more than to simply acknowledge that there is one God. The Bible says that "even the demons believe that—and shudder" (James 2:19). And it means more than simply agreeing that Jesus is the Messiah and the Son of God. "Believe" means to "adhere to, trust in, and rely on the truth". It does not mean simply joining a church or acting religious. It is surrendering your life to Christ and allowing His Spirit to dwell within you.

Believing in Christ is clearly not the same thing as saying that all religions are one, or that all religions are the same, or that all religions are equally true.

"This, the first of His miraculous signs, Jesus performed at Cana in Galilee. He thus revealed His glory, and His disciples put their faith in Him" (John 2:11)

"For God so loved the world that He gave His one and only Son, that whoever believes in Him shall not perish but have eternal life" (John 3:16)

"Whoever believes in Him is not condemned, but whoever does not believe stands condemned already because he has not believed in the name of God's one and only Son" (John 3:18)

"Then Jesus declared, "I am the bread of life. He who comes to Me will never go hungry, and he who believes in Me will never be thirsty" (John 6:35)

"For My Father's will is that everyone who looks to the Son and believes in Him shall have eternal life, and I will raise him up at the last day" (John 6:40)

"I tell you the truth, he who believes has everlasting life" (John 6:47)

"On the last and greatest day of the Feast, Jesus stood and said in a loud voice, "If anyone is thirsty, let him come to Me and drink. Whoever believes in Me, as the Scripture has said, streams of living water will flow from within Him" (John 7:37-38)

"I told you that you would die in your sins; if you do not believe that I am the one I claim to be, you will indeed die in your sins" (John 8:24)

"Jesus heard that they had thrown him out, and when He found him, He said, "Do you believe in the Son of Man?" (John 9:35)

"Then Jesus cried out, "When a man believes in Me, he does not believe in Me only, but in the one who sent Me" (John 12:44)

Jesus answered "You believe at last!" (John 16:31)

"My prayer is not for them alone. I pray also for those who will believe in Me through their message" (John 17:20).

Jesus says we can't earn our salvation through works. It's common for people to think they need to do something to earn their way into God's favor. But that's not what Jesus says. He says it is simply a matter of belief.

"Then they asked Him, "What must we do to do the works God requires?" Jesus answered, "The work of God is this: to believe in the one He has sent" (John 6:28-29).

Jesus says when we believe, we become children of God: "Yet to all who received Him, to those who believed in His name, He gave the right to become children of God, children born not of natural descent, nor of human decision or a husband's will, but born of God" (John 1:12-13). What does this mean? It means we must be "born again" spiritually. "In reply Jesus declared, "I tell you the truth, no one can see the kingdom of God unless he is born again" (John 3:3). "Jesus answered, "I tell you the truth, no one can enter the kingdom of God unless he is born of water and the Spirit" (John 3:5). "Flesh gives birth to flesh, but the Spirit gives birth to spirit. You should not be surprised at my saying, "You must be born again" (John 3:6-7).

God cares what we believe. He cared enough to become flesh and live the perfect life we could not live. Because Jesus did that and took our punishment for sin, He bridged the gap between God and man so that we have access to God and eternal life through Him.

Jesus was very real and He was not delusional. He knew exactly who He was\is and what He was doing. Jesus preached more about Hell than He did about Heaven. He does not desire anyone to go to Hell, but everyone has sinned and come short of the glory of God. Because of that, everyone was destined for Hell who stood alongside Satan in his rebellion against God.

God became flesh in body of Jesus Christ in order to redeem us from death and Hell and eternal separation from Him. Jesus made it clear that He was the only way to get to Heaven. He said, anyone who tried to get there any other way were thieves and liars and had no part in the Kingdom of Heaven.

It is not enough to "mean well as long as you at least try to learn." If that were enough, He would not have had to go through the agony of the crucifixion and all that involved, the pain suffering and torture and rejection by His own creation. But He went into Hell and brought out Paradise and those who believed in Him from long before the incarnation based upon God's word and prophecy. He resurrected from the dead and was seen by hundreds of people.

The Priests and Romans tried to cover up the resurrection with lies and by paying off the Roman guard who stood guard over the tomb but could not prevent the angel from moving the stone or all the rest that took place.

The Roman soldiers would have been killed in a horrible way had they really fallen asleep while guarding the tomb, but they were paid to lie and sent out to try to sell that lie to anyone who would fall for it.

The disciples had run away afraid of being arrested and they all went into hiding. They were in no way capable or even of the mindset to start a new religion. They thought Jesus was dead and feared they would be next.

Something dramatic happened after the crucifixion. Jesus appeared to the disciples and hundreds of others. Jews turned away from Judaism and began to boldly tell everyone the truth: Jesus lived and had conquered death. They now knew they had been in the very presence of God and they would not renounce Him even if it meant they would have to die for their beliefs.

These people saw something so wonderful that they spread the truth and people everywhere found hope and life and love. They shared what they had with others. They taught love and forgiveness and kindness, but most of all that there is a God and He is personal and He loves us.

But, Jesus said, "Unless you believe that I am, you will die in your sins."

When asked, "What must I do to be saved?"

The answer was, "Believe on the Lord Jesus and you will be saved." So, yes God does care what you believe. If you reject His son, you have rejected Him.

ALL RELIGIONS ARE NOT THE SAME. COMPARE THEM FOR THE MESSAGE THEY TEACH... WHAT DO THEY SAY ABOUT JESUS? HE IS THE MEASURE OF ALL TRUTH AND ALL FAITH. HE SAID THAT NO ONE WILL GET INTO HEAVEN UNLESS THEY BELIEVE ON HIM AND ARE BORN AGAIN OF THE HOLY SPIRIT. WE ARE SAVED BY GRACE AND NOT BY WORKS LEST ANY MAN SHOULD BOAST. IT IS GRACE GIVEN BY HIS BLOOD BY THE LOVE AND MERCY OF GOD ALMIGHTY. IF THEY DENY THIS OR TWIST THIS TO SAY ANYTHING DIFFERENT, THEY ARE DOING THE WORKS OF THE ENEMY OF GOD, A VERY REAL BEING, A FALLEN ANGEL, LUCIFER WHO IS NOW CALLED SATAN.

The very FIRST lie ever told was in the Garden of Eden. The liar was Lucifer, whose name would later be changed to 'Satan', which means 'adversary'. When God created Adam, He brought all the animals to Adam to name.

All the animals had mates, but there was not a mate for Adam. So, God created a woman for Adam: Genesis 2:21-25: "And the LORD God caused a deep sleep to fall upon Adam, and he slept: and He took one of his ribs, and closed up the flesh instead thereof; 22) And the rib, which the LORD God had taken from man, made he a woman, and brought her unto the man. 23) And Adam said, 'This is now bone of my bones, and flesh of my flesh: she shall be called Woman, because she was taken out of Man. 24) Therefore shall a man leave his father and his mother, and shall cleave unto his wife: and they shall be one flesh.' 25) And they were both naked, the man and his wife, and were not ashamed."

As revealed in Genesis, the first evil work of Satan was to lie in order to convince Eve that she and Adam could become Gods. He used pride as a tool to woo her away from the truth. His sin was to call God a liar. Her sin was to believe Satan, and Adam's sin was to fail to stand with the word he first received from God. "Now the serpent was more subtle than any beast of the field which the LORD God had made. And he said to the woman, "Yea, has God said, you shall not eat of every tree of the garden?" And the woman said unto the serpent, "We may eat of the fruit of the trees of the garden: But of the fruit of the tree which is in the midst of the garden, God has said, you shall not eat of it, neither shall you touch it, lest you die." And the serpent said to the woman, "You shall not surely die: For God knows that in the day you eat thereof, then your eyes shall be opened, and you shall be as gods, knowing good and evil." And when the woman saw that the tree was good for food, and that it was pleasant to the eyes, and a tree to be desired to make one wise, she took of the fruit thereof, and did eat, and gave also to her husband with her; and he did eat." (Genesis 3:1-6)

Later in scripture, Jesus refers again to Satan (the Devil) as a liar: John 8:44: "Ye are of your father the devil, and the lusts of your father ye will do. He was a murderer from the beginning, and abode not in the truth, because there is no truth in him. When he speaketh a lie, he speaketh of his own: for he is a liar, and the father of it:"

Satan is a most powerful angel, and he rebelled against God, and took a third of the angels with him when he hardened his heart against God. Satan hates all of mankind and seeks to destroy all. Our only protection from him is the Lord God Almighty. God has appointed His faithful angels to watch over us and help us in our struggles against our adversary, the Devil.

In order to understand just what we are up against, this is what scripture tells us about how Satan and his minions are able to do in order to lure us away from the truth: "And no marvel; for Satan himself is transformed into an angel of light. 15) Therefore it is no great thing if his ministers also be transformed as the ministers of righteousness; whose end shall be according to their works." (2Corinthians 11:14-15)

We have God on our side when we put our trust in Jesus Christ, who is able to defend us against the wiles of the Devil, and deliver us home safely to Heaven one day.

A WARRIOR'S ARMOR

In Ephesians 6:10-18, Paul gives us instructions on how to protect ourselves from the deceptions of the world, the flesh and the Devil: 10) "Finally, my brethren, be strong in the Lord, and in the power of His might. 11) Put on the whole armour of God, that ye may be able to stand against the wiles of the devil. 12) For we wrestle not against flesh and blood, but against principalities, against powers, against the rulers of the darkness of this world, against spiritual wickedness in high places. 13) Wherefore take unto you the whole armour of God that ye may be able to withstand in the evil day, and having done all, to stand.   14) Stand therefore, having your loins girt about with truth, and having on the breastplate of righteousness; 15) And your feet shod with the preparation of the gospel of peace; 16) Above all, taking the shield of faith, wherewith ye shall be able to quench all the fiery darts of the wicked. 17) And take the helmet of salvation, and the sword of the Spirit, which is the word of God: 18) Praying always with all prayer and supplication in the Spirit, and watching thereunto with all perseverance and supplication for all saints;"

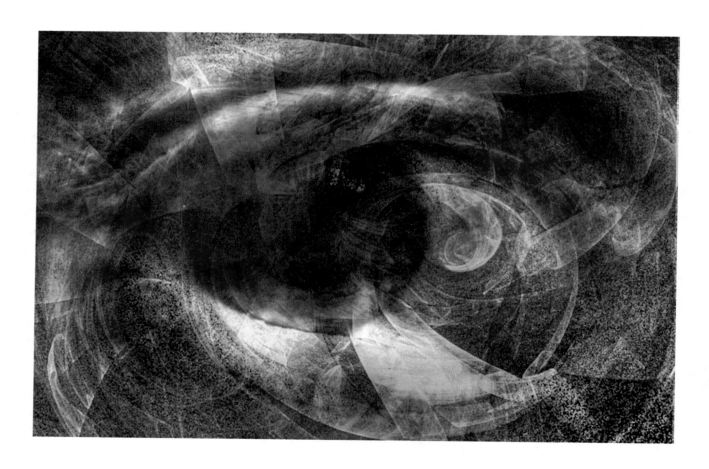

MEDITATE UPON THE LORD

Writing and visual art are a special love of mine. When combined, the two join forces to open the hearts and minds of the persons who view read and view my work. The two mediums together have a power that is greater than the sum total of the two when presented separately.

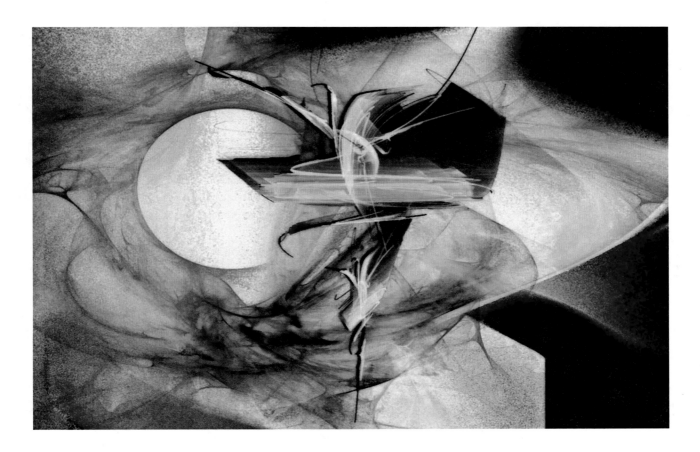

I was sitting in a training session many years ago learning all the rules and regulations of a new job. Then I found myself caught up and carried away in thought and this verse filled my very being and I wrote it down quickly before it was lost. In those days I was still searching for my purpose of being alive and striving to find the answers.

Now...I am at peace and realize that loving God is my purpose in life...and reflecting His light in my life is the greatest thing I can ever do.

MEDITATION

The unknown seems unclear,

as it draws me ever nearer.

The soft strains of lavender

melancholy memories play a light soliloquy in my ear.

In foreboding silence I

contemplate the way the moments fly. While in lingering spasms of time,

the inquisitions and acquisitions

fill the chasms of my mind.

I feel yet incomplete,

at a loss, I cannot speak,

for the words would lose their meaning

as I describe that which I see.

In a glorious flash of light,

in a nebulous state am I.

All I've learned is just a stone

in the building of my mind.

We are more than I.

I, my soul and I my mind and I, the child of God

Fill this life and share this body 'til I die.

Our brains absorb multiple inputs in ways we do not consciously comprehend. What a wonderful God we have to create us in such a marvelous complex being that even scientists cannot fully explain. Art is a gift that no one can explain but can be enjoyed by all. We are told to meditate upon God and

His works. Psalms 77:12-13 says: "I will meditate also of all Your work, and talk of Your doings. Your way, O God, is in the sanctuary: who is so great a God as our God?" Meditation according to the God of life is to fill our thoughts with the Holy things of God, not empty our minds of all thoughts which is a pagan thing brought in by ungodly self-righteous religions whose end is the path of the destitute. When we meditate on the Word of God, the Love of God, the Majesty of God, we learn to trust in God.

SOMETHING TO MEDITATE ON:

Without The Cross, there would be no resurrection.

Without God, there would be no Cross.

Without love, life would have no color.

Without God, there would be no love.

Without romance, love would lose its glow.

Without God, there would be no romance.

Without music, there would be no song.

Without God, there would be no music.

Without charity, there would be no giving.

Without God, there would be no charity.

Without dreams, there would be no inspiration.

Without God, there would be no dreams.

Without hope, there would be no purpose.

Without God, there would be no hope.

Without faith, the bird would not leave the nest.

Without God, there would be no nest.

Without Grace, there would be no Mercy.

Without God, there would be no Grace.

1Timothy 4:15: "Meditate upon these things; give thyself wholly to them; that thy profiting may appear to all. "

1Timothy 4:16: "Take heed unto thyself, and unto the doctrine; continue in them: for in doing this thou shalt both save thyself, and them that hear thee." Philippians 4:8: "Finally, brethren, whatsoever things are true, whatsoever things are honest, whatsoever things are just, whatsoever things are pure, whatsoever things are lovely, whatsoever things are of good report; if there be any virtue, and if there be any praise, think on these things."

When we meditate, we think and enrich our minds with the understanding that comes from God and is a blessing that brings us peace, not as the world gives, but a peace with God, and understanding of our right relationship with Him, our Creator who desires to have us with Him as His children forever.

A NEW CREATION IN CHRIST

I've marveled many times wondering how a duck knows to lead a flock to southern comfort and back to northern summers, but they do. No one knows how two cells can join together and change, grow and form themselves into the miracle that is life, but they do. From the time it is hatched, a baby turtle must feed and protect itself in order to stay alive, and it does. The miracle of an obvious plan is evident from the microscopic to the telescopic. To deny the existence of a creator of the universe is to put upon oneself the cloak of egotism worthy only of fools. From the moment of conception, our cells follow the design created by God, and a human being is formed. However, since sin has run rampant for almost six thousand years of human history, its results are often tragic. Because sin ultimately leads to degeneration, not only has the world fallen into decay, but also genetic codes can be damaged resulting in birth defects. When I hear someone complain of all the problems in the world, declaring that there can't be a loving God because a loving God would not allow little children to suffer birth defects or starve or be hurt in the multitudinous ways children suffer in this world, I can only remind them that these are the result of sin and self-will. It is a mindset that locks us into a false idea of reality, believing that our version of time and space is the only one that exists or matters.

I don't think there's an excuse out there that I haven't heard for denying the existence of God. But, when it all comes down, if I've got to be wrong, I'd rather err on the side of absolute truth, reality, justice and an absolutely merciful, trustworthy and loving God. Although this may not be 'politically correct,' politics change...eternity doesn't.

When I place my eyes back on eternity, I realize there is a bigger picture here than any of us can see or imagine. I can only seek the answers and not stop seeking until I leave this life and go on to the next place. During my many years of searching, I have seen with my own eyes that there does exist the reality of sin.

Sin separates us from God and keeps us in bondage. Self-will creates the illusion of self-control. We are actually servants from the moment of conception. However, God has provided a way to set us free from our bondage to sin and thereby have His strength to carry us through this life and beyond.

We do have a number of tools available to help us in discerning the truth, and one of them is wisdom. There is worldly wisdom and Godly wisdom, and the two are usually in conflict with each other. Godly wisdom considers the whole question and the ultimate eternal effect. Worldly wisdom disregards the spiritual and only considers the present worldly, fleshly benefits which are at best only temporary and at maximum only last until we die.

The following work was inspired by a friend who would not believe in God or the fact that sin has such a devastating effect on our lives;

Perhaps you know someone like that, someone who walks in pride of self, in a continual puffed up ego who not only does not believe there is a God, but one who mocks God and those who believe in powers greater than ourselves.

This man did not see himself as others see him, but was much like the proverbial scruffy cat who looks into the mirror and sees a handsome and powerful lion, someone who has grown accustomed to lying to themselves.   He liked to think of himself as a 'sophisticated man'.

A SOPHISTICATED MAN

Oh you foolish 'sophisticated' man, you think faith in God is Neanderthal. You complain of all your bad luck in life, and bounce negative thoughts off every wall. Of course, you're above superstition and things unseen with your scientific, modern mind and all.

You don't even foolishly believe in yourself,

so, when you need help, who do you call?

You say you're the world's unluckiest man because things go wrong and you're the first to fall.

Yet, you are afraid to reach out your hand,

refusing to believe Jesus could change it all.

You keep getting angry and keep getting hurt, and the more clever you are, the harder you fall.

Why do you hate and reject the perfect love

of the One who died for us all?

You say it's a crutch to have faith in God, but, aren't you leaning on failure every time you fall?

Isn't it success that you fear and hope that you hate?

And aren't you just lying to yourself after all?

Mark 4:40: "And he said unto them, Why are ye so fearful? How is it that ye have no faith?"

Mark 11:22: "And Jesus answering saith unto them, Have faith in God."

By faith we put our trust in God and become a new creation, born again of the Holy Spirit. 2Co 5:17-18: "Therefore if any man be in Christ, he is a new creature: old things are passed away; behold, all things are become new. 18) And all things are of God, who hath reconciled us to himself by Jesus Christ, and hath given to us the ministry of reconciliation;" TO WHICH I SAY "AMEN"

A BOOK LIKE NO OTHER

We can seek the answers in worldly books which is fine for some things...but not for eternity. There is only one book with all the answers for any situation and which has the correct answers every time;

The Holy Bible.

This book has proved itself to be authored, preserved, and correctly translated by the inspiration of an infallible Holy, Just and Merciful, Loving Creator who alone is able to provide for our needs, defend us from the enemy, comfort us when we're lonely, guide us through this land of darkness and ultimately exchange this decaying flesh we presently inhabit for an incorruptible, immortal glorious Being when we leave this place.

The Holy Bible is like our family album. It contains our history and shows how God has created all things and then interacted with His creation from the very beginning. The Bible testifies that there is only one true God.

Yes, there is one God. We can know it. No other book in history has given prophecies that have come true 100% EXCEPT THE BIBLE. The word of God came to men in days of old and they faithfully wrote these things even revealing their own shortcomings, their own weakness and their own sins, not trying to cover up their sins, but doing the will of God. There are more ancient fragments to support the Bible than any other writings of antiquity. In 1948 the Dead Sea Scrolls were found, and they were virtually the same as other later scrolls, fragments and documents, revealing that these writings had not been corrupted as some false preachers teach. The Dead Sea Scrolls date back over a thousand years BC. Archeology has also revealed the truths of Biblical accounts of many things including the existence of many cities and also the reality of the House of David.

There are presently 5,686 Greek manuscripts in existence today for the New Testament. If we were to compare the number of New Testament manuscripts to other ancient writings, we find that the New Testament manuscripts far outweigh the others in quantity.

If the critics want to disregard the New Testament, then they must also disregard other ancient writings by Plato, Aristotle, and Homer. This is because the New Testament documents are better-preserved and more numerous than any other ancient writings. Because they are so numerous, they can be cross checked for accuracy... and they are very consistent.

There are thousands more New Testament Greek manuscripts than any other ancient writing. The internal consistency of the New Testament documents is about 99.5% textually pure. That is an amazing accuracy. In addition there are over 19,000 copies in the Syriac, Latin, Coptic, and Aramaic languages. The total supporting New Testament manuscript base is over 24,000.

Almost all biblical scholars agree that the New Testament documents were all written before the close of the First Century. If , as the Bible records, Jesus was crucified in 30 A.D., then that means that the entire New Testament was completed within 70 years. This is important because it means there were plenty of people around when the New Testament documents were penned who could have contested the writings. In other words, those who wrote the documents knew that if they were inaccurate, plenty of people would have pointed it out. But, we have absolutely no ancient documents contemporary with the First Century that contest the New Testament texts.

We even have a fragment of the gospel of John that dates back to around 29 years from the original writing (John Rylands Papyri 125 A.D.). This is extremely close to the original writing date. This is simply unheard of in any other ancient writing and it demonstrates that the Gospel of John is a First Century document.

If the critics of the Bible dismiss the New Testament as reliable information, then they must also dismiss the reliability of the writings of Plato, Aristotle, Caesar and Homer. On the other hand, if the critics acknowledge the historicity and writings of those other individuals, then they must also retain the historicity and writings of the New Testament authors; after all, the evidence for the New Testament's reliability is far greater than the others. The Christian has substantially superior criteria for affirming the New Testament documents than he does for any other ancient writing. It is good evidence on which to base the trust in the reliability of the New Testament.

The historicity of the Bible is even greater than that of Nero, Caesar, Christopher Columbus, even that of George Washington. The list of people of history who have been accepted as having lived and taken part in the human drama is shadowed by the number of documents that are in existence to substantiate the life of Jesus and what He has done for all mankind.

The Bible has been attacked by Satan because he fears the word of God knowing that faith comes from hearing and hearing by the word of God. He uses ungodly people as tools to try to destroy the foundation of our faith, but he has failed. There remains those who are faithful who believe God and who study to show themselves approved, strongly grounded in the word of God. There is one God who has revealed Himself as God the Father, God the Son and God the Holy Ghost. He is Supernatural and we cannot explain how He can be one God, yet revealed as a Triune God, but He has revealed it in the Bible and His word is true. He cannot lie.

One day we must all leave this realm of existence and be faced with eternity. Our goal should be Heaven, complete with all the blessings God wishes to bestow upon us.

I'LL FLY AWAY

Any moment now I'll fly away, when the Spirit's willing and my Soul can catch the wind. When I drink my fill at this place and need to find another, I'll spread my arms and soar into the light. You'll look for me and I'll be gone, just a memory in your heart. With joy and freedom to brighten my soul I'll fly away.

This is the true purpose we were born, to live for eternity with God once our work is done here on Earth. We have value. God took upon himself a fleshly body and walked the walk we cannot walk, died the death nightmares are made of ... FOR US ... so that we, by His Grace, are able to receive His Righteousness as a Gift which is in fact the Gift of Eternal Glorious Life with Him. What an awesome God we have.

We all are faced with decisions in our lives. One extremely important decision is how we choose to relate to God. We can love Him, hate Him, or be indifferent to Him. If I have chosen to hate Him, that means I believe He exists and am a fool indeed to hate my Creator who is able to save me from the worst imaginable pit of despair and eternal torment, and truly wants to save me from such a fate. The opposite of love is indifference, not hate. If I choose to be indifferent to Him, then I have chosen to do the opposite of love Him which is just as bad as hating Him and results in the same fate as those who openly profess to hate Him.

WHAT ARE THE COMMANDMENTS GIVEN IN THE NEW TESTAMENT: We have a NEW Covenant with God through the blood of Jesus Christ:

We know it is wrong to murder, steal and cheat; but are there a million laws we should be trying to keep, or how do we know if we are doing the right thing? Is Christianity that complicated? Of course not! God's ways are often too simple for us to grasp! As a matter of fact, the whole law can be summed up into two commandments. Two simple commandments!

Matthew 22:37-40, "Jesus said unto him, Thou shalt love the Lord thy God with all thy heart, and with all thy soul, and with all thy mind. This is the first and great commandment. And the second is like unto it, Thou shalt love thy neighbor as thyself. On these two commandments hang all the law and the prophets."

It is as simple as that! If everybody loved the Lord and each other, like Christ loved us, there would be no sin in the world! There would be no murder, no hate, no bitterness, no adultery, no stealing nor any other kind of sin, if we only loved the Lord with all our heart and our neighbor as our own self!

Do onto others...

Matthew 7:12, "Therefore all things whatsoever ye would that men should do to you, do ye even so to them: for this is the law and the prophets."

That's right! Whatever you do to others, ask yourself, "Would I like them to do this to me?" Is that such a hard rule to live by?

Love CANNOT get you into heaven

But, though true love is the core of how we should treat others, it is NOT what gets a person into heaven. How can love take away our sins? It can't, only Jesus can do that, and our only way to receive forgiveness is to believe upon Him.

The core of our salvation depends on our belief in Jesus, as He is the Son of God and He died on the cross for our sins.

"He that believeth on Him is not condemned: but he that believeth not is condemned already, because he hath not believed in the name of the only begotten Son of God." (John 3:18)

Love is important, and God puts that love in our hearts when we put our faith in Him, and only Jesus will get you into heaven!

When we realize that God is the ultimate authority, we also understand that our actions produce consequences. God is neither unpredictable nor inconsistent. We have been given clear laws to live by and to be at peace with God, nature and each other. Yes, God is merciful. However, He is also just. Although He is never without compassion, His judgment is based on what's ultimately right. When we respect God, we respect ourselves and others as well. God is the great playwright on the Tabloid of Eternity. After all, He is the author and finisher of our faith. "Behold, He cometh with clouds; and every eye shall see Him, and they also which pierced Him: and all kindreds of the earth shall wail because of Him. Even so, Amen. I am Alpha and Omega, the beginning and the ending, saith the Lord, which is, and which was, and which is to come, the Almighty." (Revelation 1:7-8)

ALPHA & OMEGA

I am Alpha and Omega, The Beginning and the Ending,

The Author and Finisher of your faith.

In the beginning I was The Word

And, by the Word, all things were made.

I was The Word and The Word was by My side,

When I spoke, light out of darkness came.

I and the Word created the world and things therein,

And without The Word, nothing was made.

Heaven and Earth, the hosts and angels We created,

And, after Our likeness, man We did make.

I created the worlds and the laws therein.

By The Word, I created, We are One and the same.

I've always been and always will be,

And I love the mankind I made.

Like the wind or the air, you can't see me or hear me,

But I see you and I hear every sound that you make.

I Am The Father, The Son and The Holy Ghost,

And, thru time, We've watched over Our children I made.

We rejoiced in your triumphs and spiritual growth,

And wept when you hurt and shared in your pain.

I set The Laws, as a guide for the world,

To keep order and balance, the foundation was laid.

And, when man could not listen and follow The Laws,

I became flesh and, thru Me, your debt has been paid.

I Am The Light, The Truth, and The Way.

I AM The Door that leads to life, The One and only way.

I Am The Alpha and Omega, The First and The Last,

I Am the Author and Finisher of your faith.

WHAT HOLDS YOUR LIFE TOGETHER?

He made the things we can see and the things we can't see-such as thrones, kingdoms, rulers, and authorities in the unseen world. Everything was created through Him and for Him. He existed before anything else, and He holds all creation together. Colossians 1:16

Have you ever considered what holds you together? The bible says that Christ holds all creation together. We are part of His creation therefore He holds you together.

Scientists have discovered a protein type molecule called Laminin. This is what holds us all together. It literally holds our skin, organs, and everything else in our body in place. It is literally the glue of our

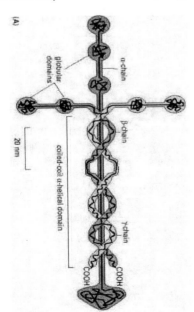

body. Without Laminin we would just collapse and be a blob on the floor. But God holds his creation together, isn't it fantastic to know that we are in God's hands and not the hands of another human.

What does Laminin look like? This is a scientific diagram of Laminin; The shape of a cross.

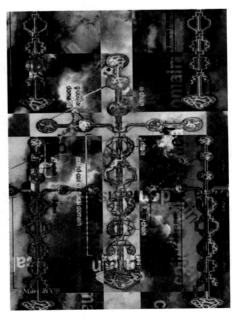

The image on the left is scientific image. The one on the right is inspired by the handiwork of God.

Laminin is an Important Protein that Looks Like a Cross. Laminin is a type of protein that essentially holds us and animals together (in very laymen terms).

Christians are making the connection of the cross shape of Laminin with Jesus Christ who HOLDS all things together. Colossians 1:15-17 states, "He is the image of the invisible God, the firstborn over all creation. For by Him all things were created; things in heaven and on earth, visible and invisible, whether thrones or powers or rulers or authorities; all things were created by him and for him. He is before all things, and in him all things HOLD TOGETHER. "

Laminin is defined by the Webster Medical Dictionary as

Lam•i•nin

noun \ˈla-mə-nən\

Definition of LAMININ: a glycoprotein component of connective tissue basement membrane that promotes cell adhesion.

lam•i•nin

noun \ˈlam-ə-nən\ (Medical Dictionary)

Medical Definition of LAMININ: a "glycoprotein that is a component of connective tissue basement membrane and that promotes cell adhesion." In other words, looking at laminin as a kind of glue isn't far from the truth. There are several different laminins.

In their book The Laminins authors Peter Elkblom and Rupert Timpl go into more detail about both the importance of laminins and their structure. They describe laminins that, together with other proteins, "hold cells and tissues together." They also say, "Electron microscopy reveals a cross-like shape for all laminins investigated so far." They went on to say that in solution the laminin shapes were more like a flower than a cross. The strands of laminins do not always stand straight and at right angles, but they do consists of arms, three of which are short and one of which is long. (Laminins (Cell Adhesion and Communication Series, Volume 2 by Peter Ekblom\Author and R. Timpl\Author)

Research has been conducted on laminins in connection with numerous conditions and diseases. It has been found, for example, that people with congenital muscular dystrophies do not have laminin-alpha2, which is normally found in the layer of cells around muscle fibers and other cells important to the structural integrity of muscle cells.

Isn't it remarkable that the symbol we hold dear to and one that speaks so clearly of our relationship with God is The Cross? This finding inspired this work of art.

The Bible tells us in 1Corinthians 1:18: "For the preaching of the cross is to them that perish foolishness; but unto us which are saved it is the power of God."

If you have not heard of this or seen any visual presentation of this marvelous phenomena, I urge you to go to youtube and do a search for ' How Great is Our God - Laminin - Louie Giglio Full Movie'. The latest full version was posted Published on Jul 10, 2013. There are also shorter versions as well. A search for Louie Giglio - Laminin (short version) will bring you to the right place (Uploaded on Jun 6, 2008, it has had over 743,000 views). Both are well worth your time to watch.

"MY REALITY VS. YOUR REALITY!"

"OR...IS A ROSE A ROSE?"

I have heard all sorts of reasons and excuses for denying the existence of God. One of the most incomprehensible one is "That's your reality." This so-called 'reasoning' claims that no one can know

what 'reality' really is and that each of us has our own 'reality' and perception that is unique and therefore, they conclude, there are no 'absolute truths.'

Many people say, "I have my reality and you have yours, and who is to say which one is real? Maybe my reality is real to me and your reality is real to you?" Some say, "If I believe in it – it's real to me." Do we have our own individual realities that are somewhat isolated from objective reality? Does believing in something make it real? Is it that, in reality, your reasoning is not only very weak, but also very wrong?

For instance, is a rose a rose because it is a rose or because someone named it a rose and, if yes or no, do you call it a carnation? If not, why not? Would changing its name, change its properties, its beauty, its existence? Are you able to wish it away by denying its reality? Are you its creator? Are you able to speak it into non-existence?

It doesn't matter what name you give a rose or any other thing. Its name does not determine its reality or existence. It does not depend on our perception of it for its existence. It exists whether we see it or touch it or smell it. The same is true of all matter, all creation, every atom and every cell from the sub-microscopic to the infinite universe.

Suppose a 'Relativist' sincerely believes that he can fly if he believes it hard enough and a whole group of his follower believes that is that he can fly. Suppose he jumps off the Golden Gate Bridge at the same time. Will he change his mind before he hits the water? Perhaps we should try it and see. We can get thousands of people chanting and cheering for him. But, when they see him hit the water and not suddenly grow wings out of necessity, I wonder how many others will be foolish enough to put his 'faith' where his mouth is. Jesus followers were willing to die for their reality. They had seen Him after He had resurrected from death. They had touched Him and heard Him and knew what reality and Truth really was. They knew death could hold them. They were willing to put their lives on the line for that reality. How many 'Relativists' would be willing to do the same? No, the claims of the Humanists fly in the face of true reality.

The point here is that gravity is real and it doesn't need you to believe in it for it to be real. Gravity doesn't require your faith, it doesn't love you, and it treats everyone equally all the time. When you stop believing in gravity, it doesn't go away.

Believing in something doesn't make it real. If something is real its reality doesn't depend on belief. Therefore, if you believe in something that is real, that has substance and\or essence whether solid, vapor or liquid and I don't believe in it then you are right and I am wrong. My belief, even if I believe strongly with all my might doesn't make it real.

If your reality is subject to your interpretation of 'reality,' then why bother to write books about it, or even try to communicate your 'reality' to me - since, by these standards and this type of reasoning, and, carrying it to its logical conclusion, you don't even know if I really exist or whether you have imagined the whole thing and only dreamed me up; Therefore, why not just re-design' your 'reality' from within to suit yourself? Just 'think' me away if you can, thusly eliminating the need for futile efforts to manipulate your surroundings by outward motions which obviously would not be necessary if you are right and if you are in 'control' of your own 'reality.'

Very wise advise comes from the Holy Bible. We are told: "… whatever is true, whatever is honorable, whatever is just, whatever is pure, whatever is lovely, whatever is commendable, if there is any excellence, if there is anything worthy of praise, think about these things." (Philippians 4:8)

We have a fleshly body, called the 'natural' body and we have a spiritual body. There are things we cannot perceive or understand in the fleshly body. The Holy Bible confirms this as revealed by our Creator: "The natural person does not accept the things of the Spirit of God, for they are folly to him, and he is not able to understand them because they are spiritually discerned." (1 Corinthians 2:14) Within context of the scripture we can get a better understanding of what is being said: Beginning with 1Corinthians 2:9, we read: "But as it is written, Eye has not seen, nor ear heard, neither have entered into the heart of man, the things which God has prepared for them that love him."

These things have already been prepared for those who believe God and rely on Him for their reality and their understanding of life and the meaning of it. 1Corinthians 2:10 reveals a marvelous thing God has in store for us. It tells us: "But God has revealed them to us by his Spirit: for the Spirit searches all things, yes, the deep things of God." These have been prepared by a being whom we cannot even fathom in our finite fleshly minds. It is impossible for the fleshly mind to comprehend a being who created everything from the tiniest molecule to the vast universe, and that this same creator loves us enough to become one of us and suffer a tormenting death to bring us back into fellowship with Him; to end our separation from what He ultimately has created for us when we are changed from this flesh into the eternal Children of God.

1Corinthians 2:11-13 describes our current worldly state of mind which God changes by our regeneration in the spirit: "For what man knows the things of a man, save the spirit of man which is in him? even so the things of God no man knows, but the Spirit of God. Now we have received, not the spirit of the world, but the spirit which is of God; that we might know the things that are freely given to us of God. Which things also we speak, not in the words which man's wisdom teaches, but which the Holy Ghost teaches; comparing spiritual things with spiritual."

While we are living in a state without the Holy Spirit, we cannot understand the things that are spiritual. 1Corinthians 2:14-15 explains it from God's perspective: "But the natural man receives not the things of the Spirit of God: for they are foolishness to him: neither can he know them, because they are spiritually discerned. But he that is spiritual judges all things, yet he himself is judged by no man.

We are told in 1Corinthians 2:16 that we must be instructed by having the spirit of Christ abiding in us to understand the very real world that exists and cannot be seen in the flesh: "For who has known the mind of the Lord, that He may instruct him? But we have the mind of Christ."

The day will come when this flesh will be changed and we will pass from corruptible flesh into an incorruptible body that can never die. The Apostle Paul tells us in 1Corinthians:15:51-54: "Behold, I show you a mystery; we shall not all sleep, but we shall all be changed, in a moment, in the twinkling of an eye, at the last trump: for the trumpet shall sound, and the dead shall be raised incorruptible, and

we shall be changed.

For this corruptible must put on incorruption, and this mortal must put on immortality.

So when this corruptible shall have put on incorruption, and this mortal shall have put on immortality, then shall be brought to pass the saying that is written, Death is swallowed up in victory."

In the last days, Satan will attack the very name of Jesus.

He Will Attack The Prince Of God - Dan. 8:25 - Here, we are told that this Man of Sin will stand up against the "Prince of Princes." This is none other than the Lord Jesus Christ! It appears that anything having to do with godliness, holiness or Christ will be the focus of the attacks of this madman. He will make every effort to stamp out the name of Jesus from the face of the earth.

This attitude is already being manifested in our day. When was the last time you heard someone use the name of Allah as a curse word? When did you hear someone in a fit of anger make use of the name of Buddha. When was the last time you heard your favorite actor take the word "damn" and place the name of Krishna before it? The fact is, you haven't! And you won't! The name that is attacked with alarming frequency is the name of Jesus!

I hear that blessed name used as a byword by a Christ-rejecting world and it makes me sick to my stomach. You might as well face it, the Devil hates the name of Jesus! He will hate it and he will attempt to discredit it and destroy it until he is cast away in to Hell's flames.

Why is it that Jesus, and His doctrines, are the most hated things in the world? Because if men admit the fact that He is Lord, that He died and rose again, that He is in fact the Savior. Then man must admit that he is a sinner or be doomed to Hell. If the Bible is right about Jesus, then it stands to reason that it is right about everything else as well. The world hates His name because it points out their sins!

Though we cannot see all things, we know by life experience that there are things we cannot explain by the five senses of the flesh. Yet, these things are real and exist whether anyone believes it or not.

The existence of the reality of the spirit does not depend on our perception of it or not. It is reality. This delusion that claims there is no 'absolute truth' is yet another lie of Satan. It is another tool being used to deceive those who are seeking excuses for their rebellion against God.

When the Bible says that Satan is the "god of this world," it is not saying that he has ultimate authority. It is conveying the idea that Satan rules over the unbelieving world in a specific way. In the case of 2 Corinthians 4:4, the unbeliever follows Satan's agenda. According to 2 Corinthians 4:4, the "god of this world has blinded the minds of unbelievers, so that they cannot see the light of the gospel of the glory of Christ." Satan's agenda includes pushing a false philosophy onto the unbelieving world - a false philosophy that blinds the unbeliever from the truth of the Gospel. Satan's philosophies are the fortresses in which people are imprisoned, needing to be set free and brought captive to Christ in obedience to the truth.

THRU MY EYES

What was life that I should seek...to watch
or live or submit a thought of what I see,
that thru my eyes might be shown some
small victory over the trials and challenges
that came my way, while as a pilgrim I
passed this way, and left a note or message
to say, "Don't give up or be dismayed
But stand up and be counted I pray,
and know your life was meant to be,
and make it leave an
indelible memory on all you touch
and all to whom you speak...
Like a stone...into a still pond thrown and
sinks...
makes waves that continue on
until a distant shore they reach."

ABSOLUTE TRUTH - INFLEXIBLE REALITY

"Absolute truth" is defined as inflexible reality: fixed, invariable, unalterable facts. For example, it is a fixed, invariable, unalterable fact that there are absolutely no square circles and there are absolutely no round squares.

Absolute Truth vs. Relativism

While absolute truth is a logical necessity, there are some religious orientations (atheistic humanists, for example) who argue against the existence of absolute truth.

Humanism's exclusion of God necessitates moral relativism. Humanist John Dewey (1859-1952), co-author and signer of the Humanist Manifesto 1 (1933), declared, "There is no God and there is no soul. Hence, there are no needs for the props of traditional religion. With dogma and creed excluded, then immutable truth is also dead and buried. There is no room for fixed, natural law or moral absolutes." Humanists believe one should do, as one feels is right.

There are many sincere people who believe that they want to do right, but they want to decide for themselves what is good and evil. The consequences are deadly. Proverbs 14:12 says: "There is a way which seems right to a man, but the end thereof are the ways of death." God tells us in Proverbs 3:5-7 to trust wholeheartedly in the Lord Jesus Christ, and not to lean upon our own understanding; to fear God and depart from evil, and not to be wise in our own eyes.

The book of Psalms in the Bible speaks of this kind of person thousands of years before the humanists came into existence. Proverbs 30:12-14: "There is a generation that are pure in their own eyes, and yet is not washed from their filthiness. There is a generation, O how lofty are their eyes! and their eyelids are lifted up. There is a generation, whose teeth are as swords, and their jaw teeth as knives, to devour the poor from off the earth, and the needy from among men." This is how this type of thinking sinks mankind into deeper moral depravity.

People have turned to doctrines of men, myriads of books of so-called "higher-learning" inspired by a host of fallen angels, led by Satan, the greatest of the rebels against God. He fills the minds and hearts of ungodly people and the bookshelves overflow with his lies. Satan uses confusion to destroy the minds of those who will not believe God. 1Corinthians 14:33 gives us that assurance: "For God is not the author of confusion, but of peace, as in all churches of the saints.

WHAT IS REAL?

There is nothing new under the sun. This has happened in the past. Only, today, it is worldwide and involves every person on our planet. Most of the world today has returned to the same condition that Israel was in during the time of the judges. This statement in Judges 17:6 and 21:25 is not a positive statement about Israel, but a negative one. This sin of "doing that which was right in their own eyes" was what accounted for the sin of Micah in continuing in idol worship. There were no judges in the land to point out this sin or restrain the people from it. The law of God had been forsaken and replaced with subjectivism. This is exactly what we are seeing today in our postmodern, relativist culture. Many within Christianity today is being remade in the image of imaginations of men (Rom. 1:21). The rules are being set by false teachers, and the Christian masses are quick to follow. We are told to beware of false prophets.

Only those who study the word of God and listen to the Holy Spirit and turn away from the false doctrines that are permeating the world will be able to discern the truth from the lies in these last days. Those who are born again of the Holy Spirit will have biblical discernment and will be saved in this age of apostasy.

Jesus makes it perfectly clear what God expects of us in order for us to enter into Heaven: John 3:3-6: "Jesus answered and said unto him, Verily, verily, I say unto thee, Except a man be born again, he cannot see the kingdom of God. Nicodemus saith unto him, How can a man be born when he is old? can he enter the second time into his mother's womb, and be born? Jesus answered, Verily, verily, I say unto thee, except a man be born of water and of the Spirit, he cannot enter into the kingdom of God. That which is born of the flesh is flesh; and that which is born of the Spirit is spirit."

1Peter 1:23-24: "Being born again, not of corruptible seed, but of incorruptible, by the word of God, which liveth and abideth forever. For all flesh is as grass, and all the glory of man as the flower of grass. The grass withereth, and the flower thereof falleth away: But the word of the Lord endureth forever. And this is the word which by the gospel is preached unto you."

ABSOLUTE TRUTH - A LOGICAL NECESSITY

You can't logically argue against the existence of absolute truth. To argue against something is to establish that a truth exists. You cannot argue against absolute truth unless an absolute truth is the basis of your argument. Consider a few of the classic arguments and declarations made by those who seek to argue against the existence of absolute truth... Proverbs 14:12: "There is a way which seemeth right unto a man, but the end thereof are the ways of death."

STANDING ON SINKING SAND - FALSE PREMISES – ARGUMENTS OF THE RELATIVISTS EXAMINED

1. "There are no absolutes." First of all, the relativist is declaring there are absolutely no absolutes. That is an absolute statement. The statement is logically contradictory. If the statement is true, there is, in fact, an absolute - there are absolutely no absolutes. Under the scrutiny of logic, the false beliefs of the 'relativist' mind is shattered.

2. "Truth is relative." Again, this is an absolute statement implying truth is absolutely relative. Besides positing an absolute, suppose the statement was true and "truth is relative." Everything including that statement would be relative. If a statement is relative, it is not always true. If "truth is relative" is not always true, sometimes truth is not relative. This means there are absolutes, which means the above statement is false. When you follow the logic, relativist arguments will always contradict themselves.

SHATTERED

3. "Who knows what the truth is, right?" In the same sentence the speaker declares that no one knows what the truth is, then he proceeds to ask those who are listening to affirm the truth of his statement.

4. "No one knows what the truth is." The speaker obviously believes his statement is true. If his statement is true, then he has taken the stand on behalf of an "Absolute Truth." Hypocrites! Like fragile glass, their argument crumbles under the microscope of logic.

ABSOLUTE TRUTH - MORALITY

Morality is a facet of absolute truth. Thus, relativists often declare, "It's wrong for you to impose your morals on me." By declaring something is wrong, the relativist is contradicting himself by imposing his morals upon you.

You might hear, "There is no right, there is no wrong!" You must ask, is that statement right or wrong?

If you catch a relativist in the act of doing something they know is absolutely wrong, and you try to point it out to them, they may respond in anger, "Truth is relative! There's no right and there's no wrong! We should be able to do whatever we want!" If that is a true statement and there is no right and there is no wrong, and everyone should be able to do whatever they want, then why have they become angry? What basis do they have for their anger? You can't be appalled by an injustice, or anything else for that matter, unless an absolute has somehow been violated.

Relativists often argue, "Everybody can believe whatever they want!" It makes us wonder, why are they arguing? We find it amusing that relativists are the ones who want to argue about relativism.

If you attempt to tell a relativist the difference between right and wrong, you will no doubt hear, "None of that is true! We make our own reality!" If that's true, and we all create our own reality, then our statement of moral accountability is merely a figment of the relativist's imagination. If a relativist has a problem with a statement of absolute morality, the relativist should take the issue up with himself.

ABSOLUTE TRUTH - THE CONCLUSION

We all know there is absolute truth. It seems the more we argue against it, the more we prove its existence. Reality is absolute whether you feel like being cogent or not. Philosophically, relativism is contradictory. Practically, relativism is anarchy. The world is filled with absolute truth.

A relativist maintains that everyone should be able to believe and do whatever he wants. Of course, this view is emotionally satisfying, until that person comes home to find his house has been robbed, or someone seeks to hurt him, or someone cuts in front of him in line. No relativist will come home to find his house robbed and say, "Oh, how wonderful that the burglar was able to fulfill his view of reality by robbing my house. Who am I to impose my view of right and wrong on this wonderful burglar?" Quite the contrary, the relativist will feel violated just like anyone else. And then, of course, it's OK for him to be a relativist, as long as the "system" acts in an absolutist way by protecting his "unalienable rights."

In order to understand absolute or universal truth, we must begin by defining truth. Truth, according to the dictionary, is "conformity to fact or actuality; a statement proven to be or accepted as true." Some people would say that there is no true reality, only perceptions and opinions. Others would argue that there must be some absolute reality or truth.

The Bible tells us this: "And you shall know the truth, and the truth shall make you free." (John 8:32) Jesus Christ claimed to BE THE TRUTH: "Jesus said to him, I am the way, the truth, and the life: no man comes to the Father, but by me." (John 14:6) As I read Dr. Paterson Smyth's book, 'The Bible in The Making' and I came to the part about Saint John reflecting back on his days with the Lord, I was moved to tears as I realized the heartache he must have felt being the last of the twelve left alive.

John's mind must have relived all the precious moments they all spent together while the Lord was with them during His ministry prior to His crucifixion, moments with Him in the Garden of Gethsemane before His arrest.

John called himself the apostle that Jesus loved, remembering back to those moments when just he and the other eleven were gathered around the Lord and he would lay his head upon Jesus' shoulder. How many times John must have longed to do that again as he waited, growing old on the Isle of Patmos. Realizing who Jesus really was must have left John with a bittersweet longing to be with Him again. Life on this earth could only pale by comparison to the brief time he walked with God in the flesh...and now waited to go the place which was being prepared for him. How many times he must have wondered why he of all the apostles was the last to get to go home.

But God had a special plan for John's life...just as He has for each of us. No, we may never be used in such a magnificent way as John was, or indeed any of the other apostles. But, just as one tiny bird can lead a whole flock home, two cells sharing information can create a whole body, so too can we lead someone home, share what we know to help someone become whole. Our lives can and do have meaning...and eternal rewards or consequences ...depending on our willingness to follow God's will for our lives and set aside a self-centered self-willed attitude.

John had been just a young boy when he began to follow Jesus. He had seen Jesus in His humanity, in His suffering and in His victory.

This man John neither boasted nor complained of his sufferings or his trials, but kept his eyes and his heart on Jesus.

A HEART FOR GOD

For John, this meant spending his last earthly days as an exile on the Isle of Patmos, banished for his faithful service to God, finally to die in Ephesus.

A lump swelled up in my chest and my lip quivered as I dabbed at the tears running down my cheeks. I was in a restaurant reading as I waited for my lunch. I could scarcely maintain my composure. Several times I closed the book and set it aside allowing

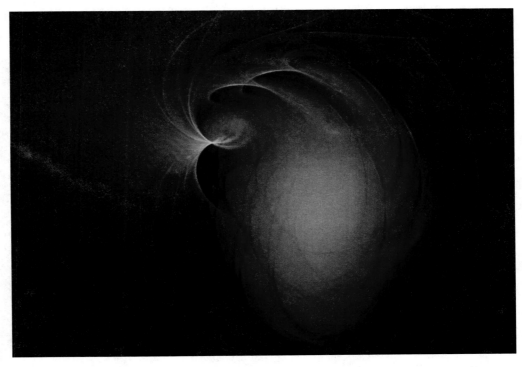

myself to remain somewhat poised considering the public surroundings. I put my dark glasses on for a moment and tried to think of something else, but my mind kept returning to what I had just read. No one noticed, however, and after a few minutes I opened up the book again.

The scenes were even more vivid as I envisioned the elderly Saint John recounting his younger days to the eager Christians who hungered for a taste of his words which fed their blossoming faith and spread the truth throughout the world.

I thought about my own search for the truth, the struggles, tears and pain along the journey. I recalled a night in my own life when I had been faced with a choice to continue in self-will or yield to a better way. So many years had passed since that night so long ago when I sat weeping in a crumpled heap amid the rubble of my life.

All around me at the time, Satan's demons raged a war as real as any Viet Nam while God's angels fought to keep me alive. I wanted to die. My spirit was in battle and I wanted to die.

The enemy took the form of fear, poverty, anguish, remorse, guilt, hatred, self-pity, loneliness, pain, grief, heavy burdens, sickness (both mental and physical), turmoil, confusion, anger, hopelessness, frustration, helplessness, prescription and non-prescription drugs and alcohol.

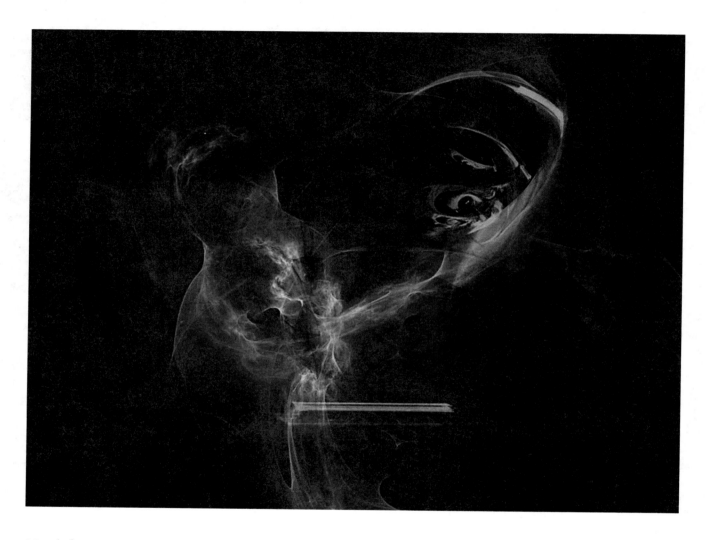

My defenses were God's ever abiding love for me and His unwillingness to let me go, His word which He had sown in my heart and His ability to make it grow, His book which was within arms distance filled with the wisdom I needed to know, His Spirit which reached out to me in patience, and very importantly... my mother's prayers and her faith that God was not only real but also cared for each and every one us even more than our own earthly parents do.

Ephesians 6:10 says, "Be strong in the Lord, and in the power of His might." I did not know my Bible well enough to know that yet, but I poured out my soul to God in repentant prayer and sorrow and gave my pain over to Him. I cast my burdens at His feet and pleaded with Him for help. I asked Him to change me, to change my life. I confessed that I had truly made a mess of my life and did not know what to do. I gave my life to Him. I was broken and He held me together. I felt naked, stripped of all my defenses.

I picked up the Bible and opened it and my eyes went to, "Ask and ye shall receive, seek and ye shall find, knock and it shall be opened." I cried out...tears poured like torrents of rain...I gave it my all, "I'm asking, forgive me Jesus for my sins. Help me, please. I seek you. Show me You in my life, somehow, please. Show me the way. Show me the truth. You said knock...I am knocking. Come into my heart, into my life, into my body, my soul, my mind, my whole being. Please share my life with me." I pleaded for hours. I read more...then wept and prayed again.

I didn't know it then, but He began dressing me in the warrior's armour, which is defined in the Holy Bible, Ephesians chapter six. I didn't realize it until later that He had already dressed me in His righteousness and pure white heavenly linen many years before that when, as a little child of nine or ten, I had accepted His invitation and believed in Him and loved Him and was chosen by Him. Unfortunately, I had taken the long way home and still had a long ways to go in my journey.

God was wrapping me about with truth, and He was covering me with the breastplate of righteousness, not my own, but a better one, the righteousness of Jesus. I read more and prayed and He put the gospel of peace on my feet. I felt His peace in my heart. Faith was given to me and it overcame the demon's attacks for the moment. The Word of God was in my hand and in my heart. However, the battle was just beginning to heat up, but now I was armed.

Now I was fully dressed and ready to stand up and fight. I knew that I was saved from the pits of Hell. My helmet was in place. The Spirit filled me and my sword was sure. I had the Word of God in my hand and in my heart. However, the battle was just beginning to heat up. But now I was armed. He had taught me to pray.

I wish I could say it was all downhill from there, but it wasn't. Like a lump of charcoal, God has been allowing the pressure to change me into the diamond He wants me to be. There are still a lot of rough edges to chip away before I can really begin to properly reflect His light the way I should, but I'm in the battle and I'm willing.

Yes, I have taken the long way home and still have a long way to go in my journey to be sure. It's taken all these years since then and many more battles have raged, but He's kept His promise and His Word is true, "I will never leave thee nor forsake thee."

FAITH

Faith is being sure of what we hope for & certain about what we do not see. Hebrews 11:1 states..."faith is the substance of things hoped for, the evidence of things not seen." Faith is believing in the substance of the thing itself even before it becomes a reality, manifests itself physically.

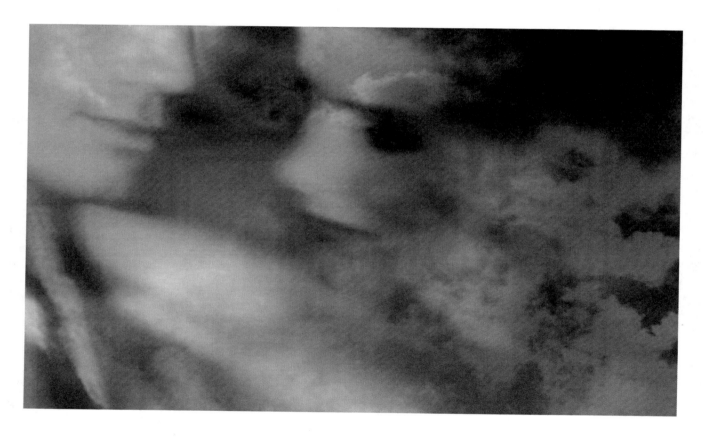

Matthew 8:13 states, "As you have believed, so be it done unto you." Make no mistake about it; whatsoever the mind of man can conceive can also get him into a great deal of trouble. While it is true that we possess tremendous unrealized potential, we fall flat on our face when we become self-willed. When we begin to convince ourselves that we have unlimited fundamental inner powers, we leave ourselves wide open for deception from within and without.

IN THE IMAGE OF GOD

Genesis tells us that God made man in his image. Genesis 1:26: "And God said, Let us make man in our image, after our likeness: and let them have dominion over the fish of the sea, and over the fowl of the air, and over the cattle, and over all the earth, and over every creeping thing that creepeth upon the earth." Genesis 1:27: "So God created man in his own image, in the image of God created He him; male and female created He them."

God gave us a will of our own and the ability to make decisions and freedom to choose right from wrong. Man's will, its training and its use constitute the foundation of all his endeavors. There are two reasons for this: The first is the will's central position in man's personality and its ultimate connection with the core of his being...his very self. The second lies in the will's function in deciding what is to be done, in applying all the necessary means for its realization and persisting in the task in the face of all obstacles and difficulties.

Herein lies the problem. The true function of the will is not to act against the personality drives to 'force' the accomplishments of one's purposes. Properly used the will has a 'directive' and 'regulatory' function; it balances and constructively utilizes all the activities and energies of the human being without bringing about physical or spiritual harm to the individual. There is a phenomenology of the will in action, that is characteristic of (strong) willers. However, the greatest strong willer ever to live was Jesus Christ. Yet, when faced with not only the choice but also the ability to change His own destiny by His own will power (being God in the flesh) He placed Himself in submission to God the Father when He prayed, "Not my will, but thine..." Being fully human and fully God, Jesus set aside His own will and fully submitted to the will of God the Father. This is not something we can truly understand yet, not in the flesh, but we will one day know when we go home to Him. Jesus lived the perfect life that none of us can live, having the perfect mind that none of us have, being the perfect man that no one else has ever been, Jesus Christ 100% God and 100% man (fathom that if you can...but then you're not God nor am I nor shall we ever be) placed His will as Son of Man under submission to God the Father for our sakes...thereby overcoming self-will and accomplishing the greatest thing ever to be done in the world. Because of his complete willingness to be led by God the Father while in his position as Son of Man, death had no power over Him, no hold on Him...He rose from the dead, not as a zombie, but changed into his full Glory as God, King of Kings, Lord of Lords. As remarkable as that is, even more remarkable is the fact that He is willing to share His throne with us...if we are willing to believe God and be led by Him.

Matthew 17:20 states, "If you have faith as a grain of mustard seed...nothing shall be impossible unto you." A wise person aligns his or her faith and will to coincide with God's will and principles which are clearly defined and not a burden when properly understood and applied. Otherwise, the power of self-will can totally destroy the individual.

We read in 2Timothy 1:7 "God has not given us the spirit of fear; but of power, and of love and of a sound mind." When we align our will with God's will in faith without fear then we have formed a powerful bond that will strengthen us beyond anything we could imagine. That is not to say we won't experience failure, but we will be strengthened by it and through it and we will not be alone in defeat but will be able to recover and rebound. Fear is doubt. Absolute faith leaves no room for doubt.

To have faith does not mean you won't ever experience fear. It only means that you believe and perform excellently in spite of that fear. Fear is not created by your spirit, but by your mind and body's desire to be comfortable. Faith is always tested by discomfort.

Giving in to the fear is loss of faith.

The opposite of faith is fear. Revelation 21:8 lists the fearful & unbelievers first of all sins, "But the fearful, and unbelieving...shall have their part in...the second death."

He who doubts is like the waves of the sea, being tossed to and fro in constant turmoil. That little bit of doubt eats like a cancer at your faith. Doubt is created by double-mindedness, having two minds. One half has faith; the other half does not. A double-minded person vacillates from one thing to another, being hesitant, uncertain, troubled and inconsistent.

A doubtful person's mind is clouded, insecure and weak. "If you can believe, all things are possible to him that believes." Mark 9:23. There can be no doubt if one is to have real faith.

True power comes from understanding the truth. Pontius Pilot asked Jesus Christ, "What is truth?" He was standing looking into the face of Truth, but he could not, would not receive it. He blinded himself with self-will.

When Jesus had finished with solitude and prayer upon a mountain, He set about to join His disciples who were, by then, on a ship in the midst of a storm-tossed sea: for the winds were contrary. Matthew 14:35 says that Jesus went to them, walking on the sea. Christ knew He could walk on water or do any other thing He chose to do. He had no doubt. His faith was pure. But then, His faith was properly placed in God the Father, not in faith for faith's sake, but in He who is the giver and object of faith...because God is the power. Faith in God is healing, strengthening, uplifting. The verses continue to tell of the fear his disciples had when they saw Him and he bid them saying, "Be of good cheer; it is I; be not afraid." He knew that fear hampered faith.

Even when Peter asked Jesus, "Lord, if you are willing, bid me come to you on the water," Jesus demonstrated He was willing when He told Peter to come to him. Peter exercised his faith in Jesus when he stepped out of the boat onto the water. However, he sank when he took his eyes off Christ, looked about and became fearful. His faith was still in the process of growing. He was exercising his

faith just as a muscle has to exercise. In the same way that muscles grow stronger with exercise, so does faith.

Jesus said, "Come." Peter came down and walked on the water to go to the Lord. Jesus was his goal. Reaching him was his intent. The verses continue to say, "But when he saw the wind boisterous, he was afraid;" He took his eyes off Jesus, who was able to perform that which he asked in faith of Him...and which was within Jesus will to do. Instead, he looked at the boisterous sea, which may be how we look at a lot of our problems, and became overpowered by what he then saw. It says, "He was afraid; and beginning to sink," just as we are often being dragged down by our problems. Then he cried out (he regained his faith...put his eyes back on the one who could save him), for it says, "He cried, saying, Lord save me." Immediately Jesus stretched forth his hand and caught Peter and said to him, "Oh you of little faith, why did you doubt?" Jesus did not say, "Oh you of no faith." Rather, he acknowledged that Peter had some faith and it was properly placed. But, when Peter took his eyes off the One who could accomplish his request then that is when he began to sink.

It's the little things and how you deal with them that show how you deal with the big things. Faith is an invisible mystery and it only becomes visible to you as an individual. It is something that can be used every day. The more it is used, the stronger it gets. In order for it to be activated, it must be received, accepted. In Matthew 18:1-6: In dealing with the question of faith, the disciples asked Jesus, "Who is the greatest in the Kingdom of Heaven? And Jesus called little child to Him, and sat him down in the midst of them, and said, truly I tell you, except you be converted, and become as little children, you shall not enter into the Kingdom of Heaven. Whosoever therefore shall humble himself as this little child, the same is greatest in the Kingdom of Heaven. And whoso shall receive one such little child in my name receives Me.

What\Who you place your faith in is as important as having faith itself. Faith in faith is nothing, can accomplish nothing good and can result in spiritual death. Faith in angels is improperly placed and ultimately will destroy you mentally, physically, emotionally, spiritually and eternally. Faith is a gift from God...for our benefit. Ephesians 2:8 says, "For by grace you have been saved through faith, and that not of yourselves; it is the gift of God..." It benefits us when we place that faith in Him and His word. Romans 10:17 says, "So then faith comes by hearing and hearing by the word of God." When faced with Jesus' commandment to forgive a brother who has repented and asked forgiveness even seven times in a day, finding such a command quite difficult humanly, Luke 17:5 says, "And the apostles said to the Lord, increase our faith."

"Woe unto the world because of offences! for it must needs be that offences come; but woe to that man by whom the offence comes!" (Matthew 18:7) "That in heaven their angels do always behold the face of my Father which is in heaven."(Matthew 18:10)

Jesus was saying that we must put our trust in Him with the humble heart of a child. God is always watching over those who put their trust in Him.

Doubts are something one cannot hide. One cannot run from them. A doubt must be faced and dealt with. Doubts are problems which drag you down. Doubts are like a weight upon your shoulders, heavy and burdensome. Prayer is an open communication to God who is able to relieve that doubt and remove that burden, lift the weight from your shoulders and reactivate your faith.

The earth is teaming with riches and power. These can be a great temptation and can be used for good or evil. The Bible (Jeremiah 17:9) says, "The heart is deceitful above all things and desperately wicked: who can know it?" So what can we do, since we are human and we obviously have a human heart? God did not create the heart to be wicked. It fell into and under the power sin when man chose to exercise self-will over the will of God...which is always directed toward our good. God has provided a means whereby we can receive a 'transplant,' a new heart; when we set aside our self-will and choose to believe Him when He clearly tells us by prophecy fulfilled, by living witnesses and archeological evidence beyond dispute that his word is true and He is able to keep it inerrant in any language.

Sin separates us from God and keeps us in bondage to another very real enemy, a fallen angel...

once the covering Cherub the Archangel Lucifer, the most beautiful angel in Heaven...now Satan, who hates mankind and desires our total destruction and never sleeps, giving him ample time down through history and presently to think up ways to separate us from our loving Father.

Satan is not alone. He has a third of the heavenly host, other angels who also rebelled against God and all of whom are destined to be cast into a place called the Lake of Fire where they will burn forever.

When we are faced with the truth, that God became flesh and we believe...then we realize that He gave us a book to guide us according to His will, that He is able to keep it correct and He did indeed perform all that it is evident He did. We are then faced with a decision. We can refuse the truth and walk away into darkness. Or, we can accept it in its simplicity and at face value. His word says, "All have sinned and come short of the Glory of God."

Self-will is sin. Sin separates us from God. Self-will is an illusion of self-control. We are actually servants from the moment of conception. Our cells follow the design created by God and a human being is formed. However, since sin has been rampant for almost six thousand years of human history, its results are often tragic. Because sin ultimately leads to degeneration, not only has the world fallen

into decay, but also genetic codes can be damaged resulting in birth defects. These are a result of sin and self-will. When Adam and Eve sinned against God, sin entered the world and the seeds of rebellion were sown. Through that rebellion, doubt in the word of God, Satan began to water those seeds and his demonic hordes of fallen angels began a relentless assault upon the human race. From that original sin, the fruit of man's failure to trust in God has ripened into the world we have today, filled with violence, wars, sickness, disease, hatred, jealousy, anger, deception, fraud, lies, pain, tears, agony, death and woes that makes our existence a struggle to survive every day of our lives.

God does not give us instructions or commands simply for the purpose of playing 'Commander General' over our lives. He does it out of love, knowing that choosing wrong paths, following after destructive impulses, seeking our own self-gratification only leads to horror and loss. One day, all this will change and we will not find ourselves in this battlefield which is both physical and spiritual. When sin has fully ripened, all living beings will understand what an why sin is not a path anyone will ever want to walk again. Then, this veil of tears, this valley of the shadow of death will be no more. God will give us rest, wipe away our tears, comfort us and give us the fullness of life, share with us the glory of creation, heal all our wounds, renew us in body, spirit and soul and bring us into eternal bliss, the glory of Paradise with Him.

God has provided a way to set us free from our bondage to sin and thereby have his strength and two thirds of the heavenly host available to defend us in the unseen realm where our real enemy stalks us.

We do not battle against flesh and blood, but against Principalities and Powers in the highest of places well beyond our physical sight or worldly hearing or fleshly touch.

Jesus numbered among his followers one of the wealthiest men in Jerusalem. God does not object to great wealth, only the love of it over Him. Wherever your heart is, there will be your faith. Nothing in this world belongs to anyone, human or animal. You enter this world naked and you leave this world and its possessions behind when you exit. All that ever enters into your hands, including your very body are on loan to you and you are only a steward, a caretaker of it while it is in your possession. The only thing that you really have a say in is where you go when you leave here and whether you choose to believe God or not. The only problem is, you have an enemy who would like to keep that knowledge from you and works quite diligently and efficiently to do so.

When students attend law school, medical school or any other of the voluminous selection of sources of education and knowledge, they learn basics in a particular practice. However, the major part of the instruction ultimately is designed to teach the student how to find out what it is they need to know in order to successfully perform the basic skills, which have been acquired in the process. This is wisdom. One can choose to seek the answers in worldly books which is fine for some things...but not for eternity.

The Bible tells us that "Many are called" but "Few are chosen." (Matthew 22:14). There have been many misunderstandings of this passage. Therefore, in order to understand it, we need to examine other scriptures to clarify its meaning. The Bible is filled with scriptures that say Jesus died for us while we were in our sins. It says that He died for the whole world. To understand this, we need to realize that Jesus was God in the flesh and that in His holiness, His death was sufficient to pay for the sins of the whole world. Although His blood was sufficient, it is also repeatedly clear that this 'free gift' from God, the redeeming of our souls from the penalties of death, we must accept, and we must receive that gift. Jesus is the way, the Truth and the life, and no man can get to Heaven except by accepting this wonderful free gift of salvation (John 14:6). So, when it says, "Many are called", that is saying, "All are called" to repentance, for God is not willing that any should perish, but that all will come to repentance. (2Peter 3:9). It says in scripture that we do not choose Him, but He chooses us and has provided a substitute for our sins that we might all be reconciled to God unto eternal life (John 15:16). When we respond to His all and choose to love God and invite Him into our hearts, He bestows gifts upon us, which are to be used as He guides us to use them. "Whosoever will be great among you, let him be your minister; and whosever will be chief among you, let him be your servant." (Matthew 20:26-27).

BEING MADE NEW IN CHRIST

It is not necessary to be pretentious, boastful or conceited. These are not qualities but rather are flaws. When God takes up residence in our hearts, he begins a good work in us and is faithful to complete it. He helps us to develop mildness and patience and peace beyond understanding, a disposition which is not easily stirred to anger. However, He does not force these things upon us, but instead helps us through the trials of life so that we are able to become these things as a result of His abiding Spirit strengthening ours. With time,

we become aware of our own shortcomings and realize the foolishness of glorifying ourselves or debasing others. Why should we glory anyway since it is God who does the work and not we? If we are wise and prudent, we give Him our full cooperation for our own ultimate good.

Humbleness is a thing of the heart. Humbleness goes hand in hand with patience. A patient person endures, is steady and able to persevere in performing a task. He has the capacity to bear hardship and/or suffering without the loss of self-control or making a foolish disturbance. A high degree of patience in the character of a person imbues the individual with the ability to refuse to be provoked or angered, as by an insult; is forbearing, tolerant. "Be patient toward all men."-1Thessalonians 5:14. In patience, one calmly tolerates delay, confusion or inefficiency.

Real patience is displayed when one is accused of or suffers for something, which he is not guilty of. 1Peter 2:20 states, "What glory is it, if, when you are buffeted for your faults, you shall take it patiently? But if, when you do well, and suffer for it, you take it patiently, this is acceptable with God." Again, James 1:19 states, "Let every man be swift to hear, slow to speak, slow to wrath." A patient person illuminates the room in which he enters. There is a discernible calmness, which permeates the very air he breathes. The person is able to ascertain the circumstances with a clear mind un-fogged by fear or anxiety.

A patient person has the ability to suffer and endure without complaint, to wait for that which is hoped for with the long abiding faith that it will come. John, the Apostle had this type of patience. Tribulation brought out the best in him and he endured until the end, glorifying God in all that he did.

Along with patience comes peace. There is a peace with the world, which is not a real peace at all, but a negotiated settlement, which can be easily violated by either party at any time. Then there is the peace that God gives that goes beyond understanding. This peace is not a negotiated thing but is a result of the indwelling of the Holy Spirit. A person with this type of peace is in an undisturbed state of mind, calm, quiet, tranquil, has an absence of mental conflict, and is mentally serene. The opposite of peace is war. There are, of course, those times that our spirit does war with our flesh. However, we are not alone in this battle, but have the Holy Spirit to strengthen our spirit so that we gain the victory, which is a far better thing than to cope alone. Without the aid of the Holy Spirit, we find ourselves in a state of confusion, our minds unclear and anxiety ridden. The result of this is fear. We cannot overcome any problem when we are confused, anxious and fearful. Any attempt to function in this manner results in a fogged perception.

Problems do not cease to exist; we merely change our perspective of them. Without the help of a loving God, we may turn our lives into an every-day melodrama, whining, worrying, verbalizing discontent and solving nothing. We become caught up in a negative frame of mind, which invites disaster and repels other people from being in our presence.

A problem is really an opportunity to learn. Attitude is very important in that respect. When we have peace, patience and faith, and begin to see a problem as an opportunity to overcome and learn, we also feel better physically and mentally. When we accept that this world is temporary and that by God's Grace there is a much better world awaiting us, then we can deal better with the thing of this world. When we change our perspective or attitude, the results are the elimination of confusion, anxiety and fear.

In extensive research testing, it has been shown that only 15 percent of success is attributable to talent, I.Q. or ability. The test results showed that 85 percent of success is attributable to attitude. Of course, one cannot judge another's success by finances. Success can only be judged by whether one truly has peace of mind.

There is a fear that is a healthy fear. We are not dealing here with the fear that comes from lack of faith, but rather a healthy respect for authority. This type of fear produces respect and confidence. When we realize that God is the ultimate authority, we also understand that our actions produce consequences. God is neither unpredictable nor inconsistent. We have been given clear laws to live by and be at peace with God, nature and each other. Yes, God is merciful. However, He is also just. Although He is never without compassion, His judgment is based on what's ultimately right. When we respect God, we respect others and ourselves as well. Romans12:10 says, "Let love be without dissimulation." Let your love be without pretense or hypocrisy. Let your respect be genuine.

LOVE AT FIRST SIGHT

I knew we would be a perfect match.

You can fill me with sweetness

whenever things get strained.

You will be my pleasure.

I will be your cup of delight.

Walk beside me my Sweetness

while my restless soul you tame.

The moment will be golden,

a time we both will treasure.

For it was love at first sight.

Carry me when I am weak.

Let my eyes not stray

from the glory of your name

or the tenderness of your heart,

and let no darkness overtake me

as I bask within your light,

'til we are together.

Sweet Prince, goodnight.

We need to be neither rude nor thoughtless by mouth or deed. In respecting persons, always respect his time. Never assume that the time a person spends with you is of no value. All time has value. It is our major resource. To diminish the value on a person's time is to demean the value of the person. An hour spent with you or waiting for you could be an hour spent furthering one's financial position, increasing knowledge, doing laundry, preparing dinner, taking a bath, relaxing, sleeping, exercising, meditating, praying, making love or thousands of other things one can do in an hour. You don't have the right to waste one minute of another person's time. Value the person's time and you value the person. If you respect no one, no one will respect you.

There is no need too small for God to take care of it. God is able to care for the greatest of needs as well as the smallest. If it is important to you, it is important to God. To limit God's caring in our lives would be limiting God's power and we cannot limit His infinite abilities and powers. God is all things to us and an infinite source of strength, energy, power, and renewal. God loves us with pure unfailing love.

Now I declare before you and the world, "Greater is He that is in me than he that is in the world." I praise His name and, as Paul said, "...count it honor to suffer for Him." He is one with the Father and

the Holy Ghost and His name is Jesus. He is the savior of the world, the Messiah, God in the flesh. He is alive and every knee will bow and every tongue confess that He is Lord.

He bids you to come, give your heart to Him. Lay down your burdens and give your cares to Him. He will embrace you and cover you with His Robe of Righteousness and declare your name in Heaven. He will write your name in the Book of Life. Come to the Wedding and behold the glory of God.

Will you come and be His Bride?